THE FLIGHT OF SUBMISSION

"Today I received a call from my past as I was reaching out to my future"

COPY RIGHT PAGE

All rights reserved,

Including the right to reproduce this book or portions thereof in any form whatsoever.

For information, address Angel Ferguson's WordProcessing

Tampa, FL 33617

Copyright * 2015 by Angel Ferguson a trustee of

HOPE & TRUTH MAGAZINE

All Rights Reserved

Published in the United States by Angel Ferguson's WordProcessing, Tampa, FL 33617

WWW.ANGELFERGUSONSWORDPROCESSING.COM

Printed in the United States

ISBN9780692557167

Yesterday I stumbled against the stones of life and injured my pride simply because I refused to remove the blindfolds of my insecurities!

Today by grace I am able to move about, not by feelings alone but with the spirit of my eyes open because of the remembrance of the pain I felt yesterday!

Simply put, some actions are not worth repeating.

Yesterday is but a foreshadow of my today and tomorrow is but an opportunity I can only dream of

to do better…………………………………..

Additional Books & Works By Angel L. Ferguson

Words, Thoughts & Inspirations

The Soul of A Woman & Her Time

The Road Map To Self-Publishing

Motivation Breaks Every Chain

Morning Inspirations Segment

Motivational Moments Merchandise

Hope & Truth Magazine

Projects In The Works

You Don't Have To Struggle

JOURNEY

DEDICATION PAGE

This book is dedicated to the love I have for my journey as a writer and motivational speaker.

Thank you for showing me that the things I thought I knew, I did not!

Thank you for bringing to my attention that its not just about my rhythm & the movement of my foot steps but the echo of my voice and the T's crossed with my pen!

To my family, I love you for supporting me with a smile!

Author Angel Ferguson

EARLY REVIEWS:

Thank you so much, Your words are truly of inspiration and let's not forget wisdom LaVora Edwards.

Words I needed to hear. A Jenkins

I receive these words, thank you Angel. Keep on inspiring the world. N Hall.

THE FLIGHT OF SUBMISSION

The inspiration behind this book…..

Was it the lifting of my eyes or the sharpness of my tone Was it that I did not bow at your command that gave you a clue that I had

discovered my freedom? Was it that I could read the spelling of my name among those that were free? Or was it that I could sign my name on the dotted line, accepting the decree that had been made?

Yesterday I gained my freedom, today I shall take flight of the things that have held me captive. No longer must I report to the master of the field for he is only the master of his field,

limited by crops and grains.

Now I can go to the master of the heavens & earth

yes unlimited is His reign.

Never a slave unto man as we were created equal

but unto my inability to know I was free to live.

Shackled by my own chains of insecurity as I had no knowledge of

living outside of my box……..

With a lack of knowledge I brought myself to this side, built this one room hut of sand floors without a need of windows or a back door to ease out of in the middle of the night……….

Tied to this pot of mud stew, drinking from the mug of simplicity.

O' too sweet freedom have my taste buds taken a liking too.

Away with this bond, created by me and on to a flight of freedom!

Author Angel Ferguson

INTRODUCTION

I know that the title has the feeling of a mystery or even a novel. In many ways it is both. After recently stepping into the role of a motivational writer/speaker it became my desire to become one with the message that is being given of me on a daily basis. When this journey first began, it was with quotes and affirmations but within I wanted to give more. Quotes can become an appetizer, here we are exploring giving the main course.

There is no way that one can take on this role and remain the same. Not only did my thoughts change but a desire for change in my life became apparent.

This experience is not easy, I am being faced with the reality of who and what I was and who I really am.

This part of the process drives you to become true to your words. So many times we have listened to or read books on motivation and the presenter is far from it, I surely can not speak on the process they went through because I was not there and it was not my journey to go through.

What moves me with love is that each of us has our own path. We each have our own style of writing. The words might have a different phrase but the meaning is the same.

I have always believed in writing from my soul. My motivation to the audience are from past & present experiences. I believe that no one is perfect and there is no one simple answer to anything but God. Now that I am embracing this role, I am learning that although our parents taught us how to become men & woman, it is in the word of God that really teaches us. At 42, I am discovering my life for the first time now at a rude awakening, my traditional ways are not all of God.

So here we are, on this flight of submission no longer being interested in my way but there is this inner cry to escape the layers that have been built within my life. Now there is a want to submit to the truthful ways of God, no longer in a position of being comfortable, it's as if my life and words are from two different worlds. I want to live as I write.

We all have a journey, We all have a purpose. And once you become truthful with the plans God has for you, then you too will discover that you can't walk & talk at two different speeds & languages. They must line up unto the same rhythm.

Motivational Speaker Author Angel Ferguson

TABLE OF CONTENTS

EPILOUGUE

UNDERSTANDING WHY I AM HERE

LIVING IN MISERY

A REVELATION

THE REALITY ABOUT GROWTH

NOW THAT I AM FREE

There comes a time in our lives that we must decide whether to survive or die, spiritually that is. God has a plan for our lives and that plan includes growth in truth. There are different areas in our lives that demand growth in order for our spiritual being to come unto it's destiny. This growth is not about our natural aging process but of our relationship with Christ. Yes, there is a spiritual aging. It's called spiritual maturity. This maturity will determine my faith in the promises of God, it will remind us of His word, the bond we have etc. Spiritual maturity tells me that as long as I remain in the sprit the things of the natural will be taken care of. There is a belief that this growth begins in the heart of man then spreads abroad within one's life.

One may ask, how can I get to where God would have me to be? Then there is the question of am I following the path set for my life? Once we seek out the gifts of God that he has placed within us, then we should seek how to operate in those gifts as he would have us to do, so & not our way. For what we will soon come to realize is this, that no matter how we try and operate those gifts, if it is not his way then it will not bear much fruit.

Apart of our purpose on this earth is to sew seeds and to bear fruit, being a witness of Christ.

In no way is, my destiny simply about writing books, being a motivational speaker or a publicist, it is about encouraging others to seek Christ, learn of their purpose and to began, continue and finish their journey's of life.

Once you can grasp the knowledge that the fruit you bear is about the lives you touch and inspire, helping someone else discover the path that God has for them, then you're fulfilling your destiny.

To hold such things to ourselves is being selfish and will in fact stunt one's growth. Consider the job of the famer. He must prune back the branches and the limbs in order for the new crops to come in for the next harvest. Each season has a harvest time. It's what we do in our planting and pruning season that will determine if we have come unto spiritual maturity.

Here's another truth, the harvest is not yours. The harvest, new members belong to Christ, we are but willing vessels to show them the way. Here we come to this flight of submission! One must be willing to give up ownership of their own abilities in order to draw others in. It is not me that others are following but the words placed within my heart by Christ that they can identify with.

So come and let us explore this flight of submission together. Even in writing this book, I am letting go and grasping with you. For no man is perfect but Christ. We are forever learning and teaching and learning and teaching until His return.

THE FLIGHT OF SUBMISSION

Life is only limited

by the road blocks placed by fear! Once

you can get over the fear of living

your dreams will have a chance to grow!

UNDERSTANDING WHY I AM HERE

I discovered that I write with a cause to free my inner anguish. Writing helps me to learn about my insecurities. It causes me to understand my value and to appreciate my worth. Another reason of writing is because it is my inner voice, having a chance to speak out loud with no interruptions! I have learned to write because it is a part of my purpose. Some of the things I was created for in this world was to inspire, motivate and uplift others not just through my words but through my actions. One of the things I was created for in this life is to help encourage and motivate others to reach their full potential.

Today, I decided to pay it forward. I saw someone in need. For me it was more than about the monetary gift but that someone took the time to notice their need without holding a sign or having an outreached hand! There is something wrong with those that act as if they can't see the need but are quick to whisper about the lack of.

Yes, this is my purpose. And I must say I love it! There is no price on the words of kindness and encouragement. There is no value in showing someone that you genuinely are concerned with their future. I have come to the conclusion that if I am not adding to your life's journey than I am causing harm and therefore I must depart from your presence. My view is to add unto your growth not hinder it.

One day, my father said to me " people need encouragement. People need those words of inspiration." I am so glad that he was speaking to that inner gift in me. And that's what I want to do speak to that inner voice of others that are waiting to be called forth.

Yes, there is an inner voice in all of us that is waiting for the right ear, the right call, the right hand to say, come forth, I know you can do it! I want to say to all, stop hiding behind your fears of rejection and just be!

Yesterday, as I was on my way home, these words fell on my mind, The flight of Submission. These are a heavy set of words that can go in so many ways. My first thought was, what am I going to do with that! After writing some notes, here is what I have come to, we have brought ourselves to this side of inner struggle. When we don't have an understanding of who we are, we create this persona of what we want others to see and accept.

Yet, when we are alone and the doors are shut to the world, then the veil is removed and what we are left with is this mess of a person, trying to figure out how to make the crowd stay around longer so that we don't have to face the truth.

Here is something to think about, what if the crowd decides to stay longer. What are you going to do when the sun fades and there is no shade?

How are you going to cover up then? I find that I did not want people to get too close because I really was not well put together as I presented. I did not want them to see my flaws. I did not want them to see that I was hurting! Yes, putting my best forward so that they could not see, behind my words of I like being single, when in fact I hated it.

We train people how to treat us. If we say, I like being alone, then they will leave you alone. Here I had created this wall by the words that were coming from my mouth. Yes, it was my actions too, but it was the things I declared, knowing those words and what was going on within me did not match.

Not only is there a concern about whom did I inspire but to make sure that my words and actions are not hindering anyone either, there is a need of constantly looking for that resolve at the end of the day, only to search again in the early morning.

There are times in the middle of the night that rest or sleep will not come my bedside manner is a journal or the notepad in my phone. I am constantly telling myself, you'll remember in the morning but the truth is, I can't relax until it is written down.

The more writing I do, there is alight shown upon my faults. Thank you for bringing it into my focus!

This journey is in my spirit, my thoughts, my soul, I am consumed with this passion of writing to inspire. Never is there a thought that I am perfect or to know more than anyone else there have been others before me, those that are here now and others that will come after me.

Sometimes my thoughts are so strong, they frighten me. Not a fear of harm but a fear that such things of wisdom would come to me. After all who am I but this willing vessel?

Last night, at the stroke of 1:30 there were my eyes, wide open, thinking of my path, repenting of the times I was supposed to move at a certain pace but did not or when I was supposed to stand still yet jumped with glee.

So here I laid, praying, then on my knees praying, wanting to make sure that I am in the will of God being appreciative of the opportunities given unto me.

Thanking him for being my hiding place. Only he really knows the heart of me, even when I don't know of it myself.

Writing is about my reality.

Yet as a writer, we all experience a inner cry that will never go away. When I first experienced this inner cry to write, I was going through a lot of emotional things. At the height of my day, I would make plans to go home after work and write but as the issues of my life were compounded by 5'o clock writing was the last thing on my mind.

The reality is that although I was writing about change, it scared me to make some changes myself. Although my words talked about moving forward, I was stuck in the comfort zone of me. To be honest, I was content.

Yet today, I am grateful for that this inner cry never went away. I appreciate that on some days it was so loud, I thought others could hear it too.

My writing has always been towards inspiration, food for thought, you know things that make us think about where we are, how did we get there and if we are in the wrong place, how can we come out.

Each day there is a new understanding about my reason for being here upon this earth and about the people that are reached. It's amazing how my past is reaching out to others to make a future. There is never enough appreciation and gratitude that's within me for sparing not just my life but my mind. This passion grows daily, and just when the thought comes, is it worth it, my reply is yes!

It is worth it when a new business is started or a person's outlook and conversation is changed.

The truth is, there is a reason why you're here. Seek, pursue it. Live it. Then share it!

A voice in the wind of caution! That will shake us with a gentle breeze!

A destiny is not reached by standing still
or by words alone

but by the actions

of the one that has a desire

to fulfill the purpose

ordained just for them!
My next level will not come to me,

I must go after it

with perseverance,

eagerness,

joy,

a mind for long suffering

&

love!
After all it is my Destiny!

There was a period of time in my life that I was so miserable that I would just sit and cry or cry myself to sleep. I wasn't happy with my personal life. The businesses were growing but there was this feeling that something was missing. The truth is, who really wants to have a growing business, living their dreams and not have anyone to share it with? I had to face some hard truths, when reaching a great achievement, there was no companion to share the news with.

I mean, after you call your parents, tell a few friends, your children and update your social media status, who else is there? I had to become ok with this. Is it easy? No. I have had to face reality, understanding that I was not in a position to give of myself the things that I needed and wanted of someone else. I'm not saying that we are to be perfect when we meet our mates, I am saying that there were some issues that needed to be addressed before being joined with someone else.

Yes, this is where my journey is taking me. A journey of the realty of me. There are a lot of layers to me some that I had knowledge of, some that were suppressed and some that were unknown. This reality is not pretty nor does it have a pure definition of speech. It's disfigured but will become a rare beautiful diamond in the end as long as God does the removing and healing. For if we attempt this task on our own we will produce falsehood. We can't fix ourselves.

For so long I have tried to fit in. Trying to belong to someone or something. I always wanted to be accepted, to be apart of what' going on. Even with being in a crowd, I felt as an outcast. Never really being secure with just being me, constantly thinking that my best was never good enough, always feeling the need to give so that people would want to have me around. I was in a real struggle to know my worth. I was in a struggle to live. At some point my title was someone's daughter, someone's wife, someone's mother but I was not much to myself.

There was this inner voice, this inner person that wanted more, knowing that there was more but I could not get there. I made things look good but I was torn within. For years, I often thought about if anyone would miss me if I was not here. The truth is, I was going through the motions of life. Then one day, I was no longer wanted as a wife but needed only as a mother.

For years, I would say I wanted love, I wanted someone to love me but the truth is, love scared me. Not only did it scare me, but I did not know how to give love. My love was on condition. My love was based off of what I could give you. And if you no longer needed or wanted me, then my love was gone. Hard to grasp right? It's the truth.

I am learning to pay attention to my dreams. Just the other night I had a dream about wanting a change. A change from where I was. A change from the people I was around. A change from those that didn't want me around. In this dream God was letting me know that he had a plan & position just for me!

No matter what you're going through, know this that God has a plan & purpose for you! This dream was so real. I was working in this office, and it was as if I was being forced out. Not out of the company but out of the department. Well, let's just say it was the person's agenda to have me put out of the company but I could see another department that would welcome me. What does this mean? To me it means that there are some that don't mean you any good with no justification.

It means that you are in an area that you have out grown or that you should remove yourself from. It means that if I look to God, he has a plan for me. That you should not despair because of what things may look like. It means that the winds may blow and the storms may come and the loud noises may roar up against you, but even in all of this, there is a plan!

What I am learning to accept is that His plan is not my plan. My plans hold no depth or merit yet His plans hold life & integrity!

My outlook is changing. I am now asking God to help me to stop pushing people away. Within, I would say I didn't want to be alone but then would push people away.

Don't get me wrong, I am very cautious but I want to be real with people. I want to live as I write. When I say value yourself and not rush to give so quickly, I want to live that. I want to walk in freedom, in the liberty of being me. I want to experience what's real so therefore I must come clean and be real with myself.

There was a desire within but nothing was coming out. I was hiding behind fear and my emotions. I had not let go of the many disappointments of my past. Now that's funny. We will refuse to move forward because we are holding on to past disappointments.

Yes, we can create our own hut of sand floors with no need of windows or a back door to escape. We don't give ourselves a chance of escaping ourselves. I am guilty of this.

About four years ago, I became serious about writing. The more I write, the reality of my inner self is being brought before me, As a motivational/ inspirational writer, it is hard to give encouragement and it not affect you.

One day I no longer wanted to die, but learning to live. Some might not understand it's so confusing when you're looking from the outside at a person that seems to have it all together. It's what we do! We have this wall of security up, and will only allow some to get a glimpse inside and that's all you'll get. We never really allow anyone to get close to us. Daily I am learning that it's because I don't want to face my hurts. I can now understand, that I had no idea of my real worth. I was not able to give what was not in me.

I'm still secluded though. I needed to really become comfortable with me. My inner voice is screaming with things to write. Sometimes I say, you can't write that! But then, I know someone, somewhere is going through a fight within just like me, and they are looking for answers in all of the wrong places and wrong people.

My prayers have changed. My thoughts about me have changed. Now I wonder, wow when did you have so much to say. It's like one day all of a sudden I had this voice. This voice that wanted to encourage others, having no idea that this journey would take me in the hidden areas of my own life. Or shall I say my own issues. I am not perfect. A lot of mistakes have been made.

Grateful!

Maturity tells me

to acknowledge

that

I do not live in a house made of glass

and therefore

have no right

to cast stones!

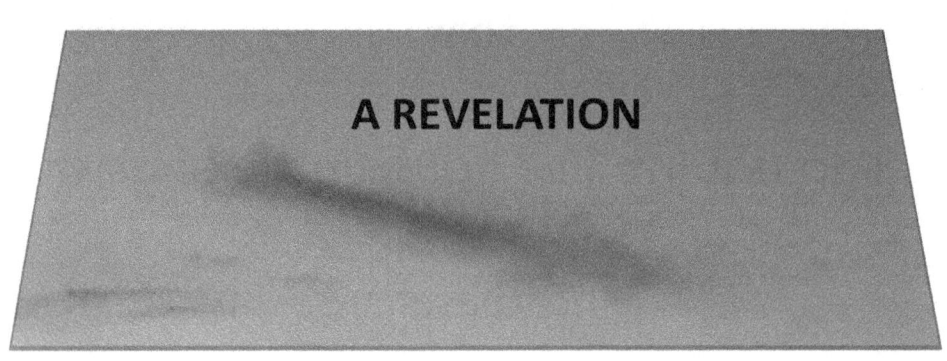

A few days ago, I came across a book title, it was based off of the book of Ruth. Knowing that I had read the story of Ruth but now that I am looking at it, it has come to me that I did not understand the words within the story of her life.

So I've been reading my bible more lately. Trying to get an understanding of where I am. Whom I have become and why am I here alone. I keep trying to add someone into my life.

Yesterday I read something so profound yet so simple. Ruth was praised because she did not look to add anyone to her life but only to work to support herself and her mother –n-law. Her attention was not on a man but on the priorities of taking care of her needs. Her life. That's a reality I had not explored.

There is a harsh reality when you discover that you are not the person you thought you were. We can create this picture perfect image when we are living within our journey yet have failed to fully remove the layers before making a fresh clean start.

I often will tell anyone that I am in love with my journey as a writer and motivational speaker. There is a price to pay when you step into this role. We must accept that for so long you've been doing things the wrong way, let's try submitting to God and doing things His way for change, there is a guarantee that things will not remain the same.

Then He will show you what it means to be a servant. What is meant to be a woman. And yes, what he meant by being a lady. What He means by being a mother, the list is endless! I must start my journey as a woman of God from the beginning!

My way has been based off of tradition and that is saying it nicely.

Here is another reality, while you are trying to get to that place where you need to be, your past will remain hot on your trail.

The more you strive to leave the childish things of your past behind the more that they will sit and wait for any opportunity to see if you have evolved.

While you are chasing your freedom, the chains of bondage are chasing you to hold on, keeping you from becoming who were destined to be!

The truth is, I kept telling myself there was something wrong with me that I was not good enough. Here I have been doing this all wrong the whole time.

We all operate by the same clock,

it's what you choose to do

in those 24

hours that matters!

I am but one person

with many hats that I love to wear!

I have been trying to find a substitute for what God provides for me. Yes, there is a reason why the title is Flight of Submission. This journey is not comfortable. It causes me to go into some of the murky places of my life.

With the title the flight of submission, it's about breaking free of inner struggles. It's not that someone else has held us captive, we have put ourselves in shackles and chains because of a lack of knowledge.

I see so much of myself within my daughter. Some of the things that I have advised her not to do, I am doing. How can she hear my words when my actions are so different? I am no better than she is or the next person.

Why do we have so such advise to give but are so trapped in our own issues? When will we admit, that hey my life is a mess and I need to figure out the same things you need to figure out? When will we learn to just to be truthful in our prayers?

When will we fall on our knees unto God and say Lord, I am a mess and I can't do this one more day without you.

When will we learn to stop pointing at the flaws of others when we can't understand our own flaws?

It's not that I am so good it's because I am not! We have a nature of wanting to ask God to correct others without asking him to clean us, remake us, mold us and to remove our ways.

Yes, our ways can hinder the growth of all relationships. There is so much to learn about relationships that I had never taken notice of before. The questions below are some of the things, that I've been guilty of. When are we going to let things grow before we start to give? When are we going to learn to stop giving when things stop growing?

Why is it that it takes so long to realize that only one of you is still there when the other one has been long gone, only to return to retrieve what you are willing to give.

This is a flight of submission! Are we doing these things to appear superior? Why not become honest and say, I am still growing. Why not admit that you weren't always at this stage of your life?

This flight of submission is not unto man to live in captivity. This is about being submissive to life. We are free to live but you have to submit to life. I no longer want to be bound by my insecurities or limiting myself from moving outside of my comfort zone.

We must learn to become honest with what is wanted. We must learn that just because we want it, it might not be good for us. We must learn when to let go.

This is not always easy. It takes a determined mind to let go and not look back. Often times, we could be in the clear but we will put ourselves right back in harms way. I am learning to accept the reality of words and actions, yes learning to accept the reality of what is!

This goes back to how we teach others how to treat us. If you keep pushing your way into spaces that you are not wanted, then you will be treated as such. This is so hard. Yes, facing reality is hard. But it's something that we all must do.

The thing about facing reality is that you must face it daily until it no longer is the first thought of the morning or the last one at night. Let's not become fools thinking that we can trick ourselves into moving on.

No this is something we must face with tears, prayers and looking forward not just with our eyes but with our heart, mind & soul. Ask me how I know and I will tell you there is an art too moving on. It can be done, if you really want it. But if you are ok with the way things are, by all means stay there.

There is this old saying, if someone tells you they want to leave your life, let them.

As my day of writing is progressing, there is caution in my wind! Forgive me for posing this question but it is vital to my survival. Why do I keep coming up with the same type of coin?

The funny thing is that as soon as I typed that question, here comes the life of Ruth again. It is because I went looking for the treasure and all the coins in my view are the same.

WOW! That is some real reality and it does not feel good.

There are two sides to every coin.
Life or death!

The caution that I feel today came a few weeks ago. But what do I do, I ignore the caution. Now the winds are blowing very hard. And here I sit trying to get out of the way of the storm that is sure to come.

The cautions that come, are meant to warn us before we become caught up in things that we need to avoid. This caution could destroy our spiritual & personal lives as well as hinder our careers.

That caution is the voice of God. The warning that comes by the Angels that he has given charge over us to keep us in all of our ways. We all have ignored that wind of caution because we figure that we can change things once we can get our hands on it, so to speak. Don't get me wrong, what you are going after could be for you but the wind of caution will tell you to slow down. This wind of caution will instruct us when to speak and when to hold our tongues. We just want to take things and run with it when you, the position or the door aren't ready for visitations.

Here is something that I have come to discover. My winds of caution come as I am in the midst of a project. It's a distraction to keep me from working on what's at hand. All things have their place but I have learned that while I am sitting idle, all winds are calm. But as soon as an assignment is placed in my spirit, rest assured here it comes. It is for me to see the distraction and to keep moving.

The journey that I have chosen keeps me in prayer. It keeps me aware of the things that I say to people. This journey, makes me become a product of my work. How can I say the things of your past are a part of molding you into where you are now, when I can't let go of the disappointments of my life? Here is where I am, not only are my children looking at me but so are those that receive the Morning Inspirations Segments seven days a week. I am learning to change right along with the words of God.

Never had I imagined when I said, yes to this path that I would encounter some of the things within. To the natural eye, we are all about image control. What people can see. But I am concerned with what's going on the inside, am I doing it the way He would have it?

Am I really understanding my journey? It's more than about writing some books and sending out tweets of encouragement, it's dealing with the lives of people. It's telling people that you've never come in contact with that there is a better way of life. And how would you know if you've never tried to experience that better way of life?

Here I am, encouraging people to love, to seek peace, letting go of anger when this is something I need to do. And it's not that easy. This journey has nothing to do with how I may feel for the moment or the day.

It's about who will hear and receive. Here is a truth, today I may write, tomorrow one may hear, yet in the end it's what we will do with these words that really matters!

Today I received a call from my past as I was reaching for my future! There was enticement on the other end. A voice so smooth and familiar. But the memory of disappointment was also lingering that made me shutter in the knowledge that it was my pattern of coming back that you were after. It's not me that you really want. It's the control of having me waiting……………………..Oh, but I have boarded this flight. And it is in the position to take off…………………………..

What shall I do? Take head to the caution before you go. Think back to what the past took and what you had to give. The past doesn't really want you, it wants the future of you. The past wants to hold back the potential of you!

The journey is not about me. It's about me being a vessel to pull someone else out as God is pushing me out. See, there is a method to this journey.

The flight is not meant for one seat. There are many seats on this mission, the question is, are you willing to admit that as you are growing that there is room for someone else or are you going to act like you have it all under control?

Here is something that has become much appreciated in my life, beautiful are the feet of those that decided to move pass their past. One of my favorite quotes it's not just the combination of colors that will create your next phase of life but the art of moving on that will make it a painting worth sharing!

You can't expect change in your circumstances without making some changes within yourself, all things must become a new.

If you can look back over your life and say its always been this way, then somewhere along your journey growth has come to a standstill. At some point you've become comfortable with settling for less than what you desire. We can desire change, pray about it, give thanks for it, speak about it but never really put any effort towards it. The ability to really want change for the better must start with the state of ones mind towards our surroundings. If you're just going to change your style of dress then there is a surprise for you, your change is just for the moment and can't stand against the tides of life. Let your change not become about how you can change others but about how you can overcome yourself. Once you can gain this concept, you will have an easier journey.

**In this rain,
the weeds will grow
with the grass!
Be mindful of what
you consider growth**

THE REALITY ABOUT GROWTH

The journey of life

is not about

a decree of perfection

but

an understanding

that we are not!

When we approach the subject of growth as a motivational writer/speaker I want to make sure that what is given of me is a reality! The truth is this, growth is uncomfortable. Growth will make some remain in their current state out fear of change or facing their faults. I can recall when I was going through a separation in my marriage that I was always angry. Not only was I angry but there were some self-esteem issues going on that I was coping with, I emerged into school. I was emotionally unavailable for anyone, not even myself.

To be honest, every chance I got, I would say, Lord, let him feel my hurt. Or why wasn't I good enough. This went on for some time. Then one day, it was as if I could not breathe. My chest was tight. The air around me was tight. I became this person that only functioned just for appearances sake, yet behind closed doors, I was a mess. Within, there was this wall that was so high in me that nothing was able to see over the top of the wall. I wanted to live. I needed to move from the captivity that I had created.

Yes the communication was very scarce but we had our children that needed both of us. And one day as I was complaining and arguing about his lack of, that I heard this voice that said "be quiet"!

This was about to become my first real experience of growth! The thoughts that dropped in my mind were to put myself in his shoes. Yes, I was instructed to consider the way he was raised as a child. You see, every house hold is different, and although some are close neighbors, what happens behind closed doors is different.

So here I was going over in my mind the things that I knew of his up-bringing. Here I was trying to understand that this person could not give what was not instilled in him. Can you see how the tables were turned? My prayer began, Lord let him feel my hurt, yet now I am asking God to give him what he needed within to become whole. My anger began to subside. No, it wasn't that I was making an excuse for him, it was a time for me to grow up and to leave my pity party behind. What we have to realize is that the other individual is a person just like us, and while we are holding onto things, they have moved on.

They might be ok with what is going on with inside of them and you have to be ok with what's going on inside of you. Here is a key in this whole process, had I taken the time to really comprehend, what was in him I would have accepted what he was able to give as a father, husband & a friend.

But let me tell you this, taking the advice to "be quiet" was the best advice ever taken. Slowly, not in my time but in God's time things began to turn around for our good. No we did not reconcile but we were able to co-parent better. The need of our children became our focus rather than the anger we had for each other.

As we continue to grow unto maturity, we will experience growth in other areas of our lives whether its spiritual or in our careers. Our children will even cause us to go through some growing pains.

We will experience hurt, and the truth is that we will cause some hurt as well. What we must strive to do is to seek peace, bringing our own selves unto the submission of God.

While we are going through trials, the thought of the other person is not on our minds or even in our hearts. Growth is about being unselfish, and that in itself is uncomfortable.

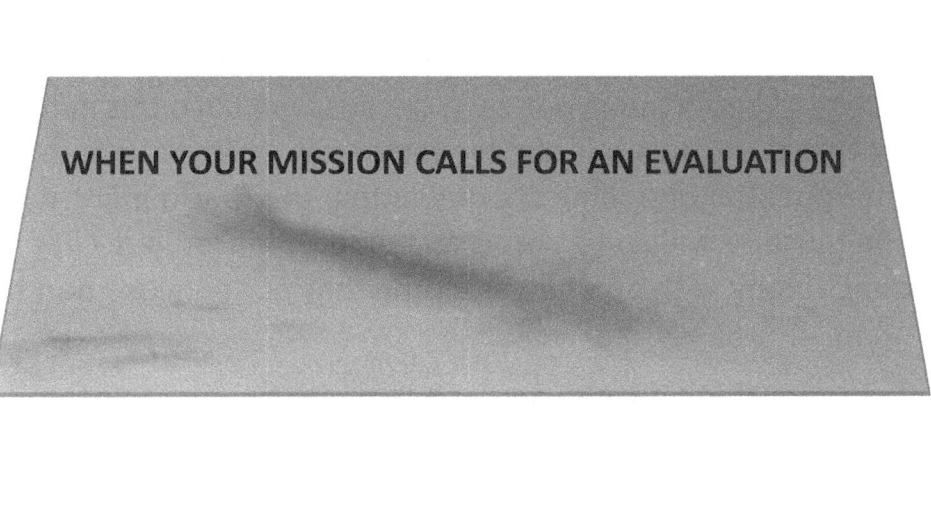

When it came to business, I found that I kept coming upon the same errors in my work, it was because I needed to slow down. If you have an employer, you might also want to consider that while you are on the job, you need to do things their way and not your way. Your way is not on the company's letterhead. There is a chance that your way is more efficient but if you're not in a position to make that call, then follow the procedures.

The same rules apply in the spiritual realm. Obey those that have rule over you. Let God take care of the correcting. I know this is not easy, because we have this mindset that I'm grown but our age factor and positions are different. The one thing about wanting to grow in maturity, one must be willing to take a seat, learn to listen & accept things along with an understanding that our opinions don't matter!

The more that I have to face the real me, the more uncomfortable I become with me. Yes, I want to go back in time and undo some actions, some words and speak for the things that I remained silent about. I have no regrets for things that this journey has uncovered. I am more at peace now that I am learning to do things God's way. There is a big difference when this journey begin, it was far from my mind that this would happen.

My purpose was to encourage others. Looking at others will cause us to look at our current state of circumstances and to make some changes. Yet, it has made me dig a little deeper into me.

At any point in my life, if there is every a notion that it's me that is writing and speaking any words of encouragement, correction is needed. Clearly, my thoughts are not the thoughts of Christ for His thoughts & ways are as high as the heavens are above the earth. One cannot teach himself. For if we presume that we have taught ourselves then we are blinded to reality, truth and are false, only to come to nothing of real value.

During the process of writing this book someone sent me an email with a suggestion of being arrogant, not putting God within the method of listing a few accomplishments from this previous year. The first reaction was in disbelief. Clearly this person did not actively follow my Morning Inspirations Segment that's been in place for 5 years. The second reaction was to take it personal. The truth is this, each day the reality of how this journey has been traveled has only been through Christ. There is not an ounce of credit on my part for all that has transpired even until this very moment has only happened because God made it possible, I've only to say that this vessel was, is and shall be willing to continue to inspire, encourage and uplift those through writing.

What has been learned and observed is this, no man is perfect. We are a forever learning creature. Yes, it has been designed that way, that no one person will know all things at one given time. For even as Christ performed things in stages, so shall we. Although my prayers, thoughts and outlook will change I desire the spirit of me to remain the same and that is too be humble.

Sometimes we can become caught up in titles and notoriety along the way, losing the purpose of why we started in the first place. When money and status become the focus above reaching the lives of people, than our ways have become lost. If at any time I may start to feel that I'm bigger than the words or not showing a genuine affection for people, than yes I'm no longer walking within my journey but trying balance myself above it! The journey of a motivational speaker is not about the money, well not for me.

If we have started a journey with dollar signs in our eyes, then our purpose is for selfish gain and will more than likely not last for long.

At the end of each day, what makes me smile is to know that something I've said or written has helped the next person in some way. When that letter comes in just to say thank you, "I'm learning to let go of my past and I'm reaching for my future", I feel accomplished.

For those days that all is weighing in and the thoughts are flowing, asking if it is worth all of this, the answer is yes. To be honest, I enjoy being this quiet individual sitting in the back ground yet speaking with a loud booming voice through writing.

This evaluation is teaching me to keep the focus off of me it's not about my mood nor a personal agenda to achieve fame, it is about the uplifting of others.

At some point within this experience, I started to take a real close look at myself wondering if I'm practicing these words. Did I understand the real meaning of these words that were coming in my heart and stirring in my soul? The answer was no! The truth of the matter is that I was not applying them to myself first, I was giving the words out before planting them within me!

We must become the first partaker of what we give.

We must become willing to take what we dish out. How can we say let it go yet hold on for dear life? How can we proclaim to smile, declaring that there is a better day when we can't see beyond the next second?

One day I decided that I wanted to live freely, my lungs were filled with anger. I wasn't living, I was existing to live.

What I failed to comprehend was that God was teaching me how to become me. Yes, we must all learn to become the true person that we were created to become not who we were labeled to be, not even for who we thought we should be.

It's true that our past is a part of our molding and grooming but at some point, really ask yourself what am I going to do with the lessons that were given?

NOW THAT I AM FREE

I have no fence to hide behind, I have to examine my words before they go out. No longer can we say that we are willing to move forward without actually taking a step.

Now that I have gained some insight on this journey of mine, I am free to participate in my life! Yes, I can make some sound decisions based off of my mind and not of my heart.

I am at a resolve with hiding behind my own shadow. There is no hiding place for me to escapes too, my covers have been removed and the blindfolds have been forsaken. In the middle of my roads I have stopped to breathe! This freedom is long overdue, thought by my age that maturity had set in. What a foolish thought yet what a wonderful process to experience. Through all of the teachings there is something that's so profound and true, those that are set free in Christ are set free indeed, it is the individual that moves back to bondage.

So here is an understanding that has come to me, just as bondage is renewed by the locking of the chains so is freedom by deciding to remain free, mentally, emotionally & physically. It's true, we can hold ourselves captive to old traditions, our own way of thinking and the ways of others. But to truly have freedom is in Christ!

It's a wonderful feeling in life when you can reach a resolve of not haggling over the small things. When there is an understanding of how one has reached a certain point in life & taking notice that things just don't seem to balance, please take the time to figure out of its right for you, if it's not then learn let go so that you may move forward. Yet become wise enough to learn while you're there. Never leave a position without applying the lessons at hand as it will help guide us in the future. Life is too precious to waste it on what could have been or if only I had done this……………! We must learn to live in the now and to love people where they are. After all we are not judges, just a contributing positive factor in the lives we have the pleasure to come across.

This journey of inspiring others is unlimited, therefore my prayer and desire is that I may never grow tired. That each day He gives me a word that will touch the soul of others. Being free is not an indication to go and do as I please but to relax in Him! It's a freedom to move about with a spiritual confidence.

You are the decision maker when it comes to your fate. There is this strong belief that if I learn of my purpose, seek the reason why I was created, take my dreams to God & follow His directions on how to bring them all into one, then I have taken a part in my spiritual freedom. Through spiritual freedom we may become an unstoppable force of inspiration to those that are seeking what we once sought after!

To truly live is within the path that has been created for the individual. My freedom is not in man, nor is it in my simplicity for my way are not the ways of God nor are my thoughts His thoughts for His thoughts & ways are as high as the heavens are above the earth. With that being said, I have the understanding that through Him, my dreams are unlimited.

As I am bringing this chapter to a close, I just heard some words that made me think and it is the best way to end this book! An inmate was preparing to leave prison and as he was collecting his belongings, another inmate yelled out " you'll be back"! You'll only go back if you decide too, not because someone said you would!

As I close each Morning Inspirations Segment,
Stay encouraged, encouraging others along the way!

Angel Ferguson

Being the author of several books, the editor of an online magazine Hope & Truth Magazine, Angel Ferguson has a passion for inspiring others. With a journey that started out as a daily inspirational text message to her children over 5 years ago, Angel has evolved as a writer of inspirational quotes & affirmations into a motivational speaker. This dream continues to grow

as the transition of a publicist in 2015.

To live your purpose, while pursuing your dreams is a journey worth sharing!

www.ingramcontent.com/pod-product-compliance
Lightning Source LLC
Chambersburg PA
CBHW072035060426
42449CB00010BA/2272